WHEN
FORCES AND
MOTION
COLLIDE

by Chris Oxlade

a Capstone company — publishers for children

Engage Literacy is published in the UK by Raintree.
Raintree is an imprint of Capstone Global Library Limited, a company incorporated in England and Wales having its registered office at 264 Banbury Road, Oxford, OX2 7DY – Registered company number: 6695582

www.raintree.co.uk

Editorial credits
Jill Kalz, editor; Richard Parker, designer;
Jo Miller, media researcher; Katy LaVigne, production specialist

Image credits
Alamy: Marshall Ikonography, 1, 4; Shutterstock: Africa Studio, 25 (top), agsandrew, throughout (design element), amskad, 5, Bildgigant, 25 (bottom), Elena11, 7, Feng Yu, 12, Georgios Kollidas, 14, Grigorii Pisotsckii, 22, karpenko_ilia, 10, Le Do, 19, Mikkel Bigandt, 15, Oko Laa, 16, oksana2010, 13, PAPound, 26 (right), pedrosala, 28, Picsfive, 26 (left), Rawpixel.com, 9, rebeccaashworth, back cover, 6, Sanchik, 17, Sergey Novikov, 30, sezer66, cover, supergenijalac, 18, Vadim.Petrov, 8, Volodymyr Nikitenko, 27, Willyam Bradberry, 20

21 20 19 18 17
10 9 8 7 6 5 4 3 2 1
Printed and bound in China.

When Forces and Motion Collide

ISBN: 978 1 4747 4707 3

CONTENTS

PUSHES AND PULLS

Welcome to the fantastic world of *forces* and *motion*! Forces are everywhere in our lives. So are things that are in motion. They are in our homes, on the streets and in the air. Once you know what forces and motion are, you'll be able to spot them easily.

A small tugboat pushes a ship to sea.

What is a force? It's a push or a pull. When your hand pushes or pulls a door open, it's making a force. When your feet push bicycle pedals, they're making a force.

The forces that humans make are not the only forces. Wind makes a force when it pushes the blades of a windmill. A tugboat makes a force when it pushes a ship. Engines make a force, too, when they push a rocket into space.

Powerful engines push a rocket into space.

ALL ABOUT MOTION

A dog chases a ball. An aeroplane flies through the air. A snail crawls across the sand. What do all of these things have in common? They are examples of motion. The word "motion" means movement.

How fast or slow something moves is called speed. To work out the speed of an object, we measure how far it moves in a second, a minute or an hour. When you walk, you move about 1.2 metres per second. So your speed is 1.2 metres per second or 72 metres per minute. That's just over 4.3 kilometres per hour.

The running dog and its rolling tennis ball are in motion.

Snails move at a slower speed than many other animals.

FORCES CHANGE MOTION

Parks are often filled with objects in motion. People throw or kick balls. They spin and catch flying discs. The balls and discs are in motion. Every time they are thrown, kicked or caught, their motion changes.

Picture a football lying on the grass. The ball isn't moving. A football player kicks it, and it rolls away. Then another player stops it or sends it in the opposite direction. Why does the ball's motion change? It changes because a player's foot pushes on it. The push is a force, and that force changes the ball's motion.

Two children throw and catch a flying disc to change its motion.

A force can make an object start to move or stop. It can make it go faster or slower, or change direction. Whenever the motion of an object changes, we know there's a force at work. Forces and motion are closely linked to each other. In fact, motion can't happen without forces.

Players' feet change a football's motion.

BALANCED AND UNBALANCED FORCES

Tug of war is a game in which two teams try to pull each other over a centre line with a rope. The teams face each other and pull backwards. They pull in opposite directions. These forces should create motion. But if both teams pull with the same amount of force, the rope stays still. Why? When two *opposing* forces are of equal strength, they cancel out each other. The forces are balanced, and no motion happens.

balanced force

unbalanced force

Suppose one of the teams starts to pull harder than the other. The forces on the rope are still pulling in opposite directions, but one force is greater than the other. The forces are no longer balanced. They're unbalanced. Motion happens. The rope starts to move, and the team pulling harder wins the contest.

A team wins tug of war when the two forces are unbalanced, and the flag moves closer to one team than another.

FORCES CHANGE SHAPE

Now picture a game of tug of war with a giant rubber band instead of a rope. What would happen to the rubber band? It would get stretched, of course.

Forces not only create motion, they can change the shape of things, too. They can make something longer, like the rubber band. They can also squeeze, squash and bend things.

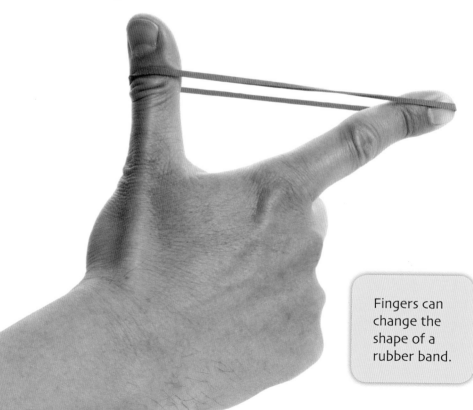

Fingers can change the shape of a rubber band.

TRY THIS!

Here's an activity to show how forces can change the shape of an object.

You will need:
a large wet sponge

1. Put the sponge on a flat surface. Note its shape.

2. Press on both ends of the sponge with your fingers. What happens to the sponge?

3. Now pull on both ends of the sponge. What happens now?

4. Pick up the sponge. Pull the ends down with your fingers and push up in the middle with your thumbs. What happens?

GRAVITY

There's one force that's with us always, no matter where we are. It's the force that makes things fall when you drop them. It's the force that pulls you back down when you jump. It allows you to walk without floating away. This force is called *gravity*.

Gravity is a force that pulls two objects towards each other. All objects have gravity. But some have stronger gravity than others. Earth's gravity is much stronger than our own. It is always pulling objects downwards, towards the ground.

An English scientist called Isaac Newton was the first person to study gravity. A story says that Newton got the idea for gravity when he saw an apple fall from a tree. Newton wondered what pulled the apple downwards. He decided that an unseen force must be at work.

Isaac Newton

Gravity pulls a jumping boy back down.

GRAVITY AT WORK

We see gravity at work on Earth every day. Water flows down a stream. Bicycles roll downhill. But gravity affects things beyond our planet, too.

Like Earth, the sun has gravity, too. Its gravity is always pulling on Earth and the other planets in our *solar system*. But the planets don't get pulled into the sun because they're moving sideways. Sideways motion and the force of the sun's gravity work together. They keep the planets circling around the sun.

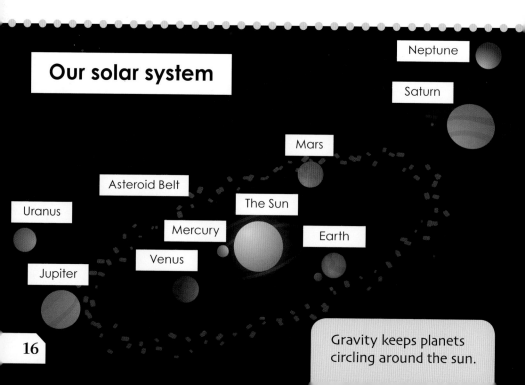

Our solar system

Neptune

Saturn

Mars

Asteroid Belt

Uranus

The Sun

Mercury

Earth

Venus

Jupiter

Gravity keeps planets circling around the sun.

What about the moon? Earth's gravity pulls on the moon and keeps it circling around the planet. And the moon's gravity pulls on the water in our oceans, causing high and low *tides*.

The moon pulls water away from the beach at low tide.

FRICTION

Push the palms of your hands together, hard. Now try to slide one palm against the other. Something stops your hands from moving. It's the force of *friction*. Friction always tries to stop surfaces that touch from sliding past each other.

Sometimes friction helps us. Friction happens between the soles of your shoes and the ground. It gives your shoes grip. There is also friction between a car's tyres and the road. Friction stops the car from sliding sideways when it goes around a corner.

Friction helps car tyres grip the road.

Sometimes friction doesn't help us. A bicycle has many metal parts that move against one another. They create friction, which slows down the parts and makes it difficult to move the bike. We can put oil on the chain and other metal parts to make the amount of friction smaller. Oil makes the moving parts slippery so they move more easily.

Some parts on a bike need oil to fight friction.

gear lever

brake lever

chain

front derailleur

rear derailleur

pedal

AIR RESISTANCE

When you ride your bike or run, air hits your face. The faster you go, the stronger the air pushes against you. The push the air makes is called *air resistance*.

The amount of air resistance depends on the shape and size of an object. On a breezy autumn day, leaves and twigs fall from trees. The leaves fall slowly, and the twigs fall quickly. Air resistance is greater on the flat, fat leaves than on the rounded, thin twigs. There is more surface on the leaves for the air to push against.

A rounded shape helps a train move faster.

Racing cars, jet planes and some trains have rounded shapes. Their shapes make air resistance small so they can go fast.

TRY THIS!

This activity shows how an object's shape changes air resistance.

You will need: two sheets of paper the same size and weight

1. Crumple up one sheet to make a ball.

2. Hold your arms out in front of you, with the ball in one hand and the sheet in the other hand.

3. Drop the sheet and the ball at the same time.

4. Which falls faster? Which has more air resistance? Why?

FLOATING FORCES

Why don't ships, beach balls and ducks sink in water? What makes them float? It's the force of water! Water makes an upward force that stops a floating object sinking. This pushing force is called *upthrust*.

upthrust of water

weight of duck

Two forces pull and push on anything on water. The forces are upthrust and weight. If the upthrust on an object is equal to the object's weight, the forces are balanced. The object will float. However, if the weight is bigger than the upthrust, the forces are unbalanced. The object will sink.

TRY THIS!

Here's an easy way for you to see and feel the force of upthrust.

You will need:
a bucket full of water

a tennis ball

1. Slowly push the ball to the bottom of the bucket. Do you feel the force of upthrust pushing on the ball?

2. Now let the ball go. What happens? Explain why.

MAGNETS AND FORCES

How do you keep a note on a refrigerator door? Use a magnet! Magnets are a kind of force. When you pull a magnet away from the door just a bit, you can feel something pull back. The pull you feel is *magnetic force*.

A refrigerator door is made of a metal called steel. A magnet pulls towards the steel, and the steel is pulled towards the magnet. As you move a magnet further away from the steel, the force between them gets weaker.

Every magnet has two places where the magnetic force is strongest. They are called *poles*. One pole is called the north pole. The other is called the south pole. Poles that are alike push against each other. Poles that are unalike pull towards each other.

Magnets hold notes on a refrigerator door.

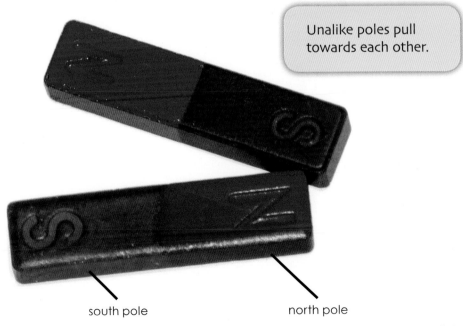

Unalike poles pull towards each other.

south pole

north pole

25

SIMPLE MACHINES

Simple machines are useful tools. They make our work easier by changing a force. Some of them make a force stronger. Others move or change the direction of a force.

Levers are a kind of simple machine. They make a force stronger. Bottle openers, scissors and tweezers are examples of levers. A bottle opener pulls a tight metal cap off a bottle. When you lift the opener's handle, the opener lifts the edge of the cap. The opener makes your small force bigger and stronger.

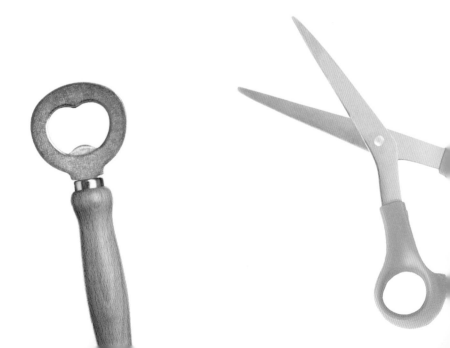

TRY THIS!

Follow these steps to make a lever.

You will need:
an empty mug

a pencil

a ruler

1. Put the pencil on a table, and rest the ruler across it.

2. Put the mug on one end of the ruler.

3. Press down on the other end of the ruler. The ruler works as a lever. It lifts the mug.

4. Now move the pencil closer to the mug, and press down on the ruler again. Is your work easier or harder?

MEASURING FORCES

The size of a force is how much the force is pushing or pulling. People need to know the size of forces for many reasons. Scientists often need it when they are doing safety tests on cars, aeroplanes and other vehicles. *Engineers* need it when they are planning machines, buildings and bridges.

We measure force in *units*, just like we use units to measure length or time. Examples of length units are metres and kilometres. Examples of time units are seconds and hours. The unit of force is the *newton* (N, for short). The newton is named after Isaac Newton.

How strong is 1 newton? If you hold a tin of soup in one hand, the force on your hand is about 3 newtons.

Engineers need to measure force to plan strong bridges.

A WORLD OF FORCES AND MOTION

Forces are pushes and pulls. They can create motion, and they can stop motion, too. Examples of forces and motion are all around us, every day.

Now that you know what forces and motion are, be a force and motion detective! Look for forces and motion at home, at school and at the park. When you see something start to move or stop moving, try to work out what forces are at work.

A girl uses force to set this skateboard in motion.

GLOSSARY

air resistance push of air against a moving object

engineer person who designs, builds or improves machines or structures

force push or a pull

friction force that tries to stop objects from sliding past each other

gravity force that pulls objects together

magnetic force push or pull between two magnets

motion movement

newton standard unit for measuring force

opposing on opposite sides

pole one of the two ends of a magnet

solar system the sun and the objects that move around it

tide rising and falling of the sea up and down the coast

unit amount that is used to find the size of something; an hour is a unit of time

upthrust upward push of water on a floating object

INDEX